The Library of
NATIVE AMERICANS

The Shoshone
of California

Jack S. Williams

The Rosen Publishing Group's
PowerKids Press™
New York

For my sister, Nancy Inbody

Published in 2004 by The Rosen Publishing Group, Inc.
29 East 21st Street, New York, NY 10010

Photo and Illustration Credits: Cover, courtesy of Jesse Peters Museum, photographs by Christine Vasquez; p. 4 © Galen Rowell/Corbis; p. 8, 22, 23 courtesy of Seaver Center for Western History Research, Natural History Museum of Los Angeles County; p. 11 courtesy of the Division of Anthropology Archives Office, American Museum of Natural History; p. 12 ©Nik Wheeler/Corbis; p. 14, 17, 20, 24 courtesy of the C. Hart Merriam Collection of Native American Photographs, The Bancroft Library. University of California, Berkeley; p.15 Frank Lane Picture Agency/Corbis; p. 26 © George D. Lepp/Corbis; p. 28 Northwestern University Library, Edward S. Curtis's 'Southern California Shoshoneans. The Diegueños. Plateau Shoshoneans.' The Washo [portfolio], plate no. 509; p. 31 Western History Collections, University of Oklahoma Library; pp. 34, 54 ©2002 Kayte Deioma, all rights reserved; p. 36 courtesy of Merryant Publishers; p. 38 Private Collection/Bridgeman Art Library; p. 40 Library of Congress Geography and Map Division; p. 41 Walters Art Gallery, Baltimore, Maryland, USA/Bridgeman Art Library; pp. 43, 45 Library of Congress Prints and Photographs Division; p. 47 X-33755 Western History Collection/Denver Public Library; p. 49 National Anthropological Archives, Smithsonian Institution, INV# 09933900, p. 52 © Richard Cummins/Corbis.

Book Design: Geri Fletcher; Editor: Charles Hofer; Photo Researcher: Sherri Liberman

Williams, Jack S.
The Shoshone of California / Jack S. Williams. — 1st ed.
     p. cm. — (The library of Native Americans)
Summary: Describes the history, culture, arts, government, and social structure of the Shoshone people of California, and gives a glimpse of Shoshone life today.
Includes bibliographical references and index.
ISBN 1-4042-2664-8 (lib. bdg.)
1. Shoshone Indians—History—Juvenile literature. 2. Shoshone Indians—Social life and customs—Juvenile literature. [1. Shoshone Indians. 2. Indians of North America—California.] I. Title. II. Series.
E99.S4W55 2004
979.4004'974574—dc22

                                                                    2003014123

Manufactured in the United States of America

Contents

A vast landscape made up of deserts and mountains stretches across southern and eastern California. The territory ranges in elevation from an incredible 14,495 feet (4,418 meters) above sea level to 282 feet (86 m) below sea level. In the low-lying areas, there are immense dry lake beds, sand dunes, and bone-dry river channels. Where desert and mountains come together, there are steep canyons and eroded hills known as badlands. In the mountain highlands that tower over the deserts, there are forests filled with lush meadows, soaring pine trees, rushing streams, and even a few sizable bodies of freshwater, such as Lake Tahoe. However, even in the mountains there are large areas of rock and sandy soil that show no signs of vegetation and few signs of life. This is a hard land with a climate that swings from fiery summers to icy winters. Winter snow lies thickly on the mountain peaks and high country as the temperature plummets. During these winter months, warm winds fill the lower valleys and deserts with springlike air. In summer, these lowlands turn into a burning landscape, and temperatures often climb to more than 120°F (49°C). During these months the mountains offer visitors a cool refuge with abundant wildlife.

The land of the Shoshone ranged from high mountain peaks to low valley deserts.

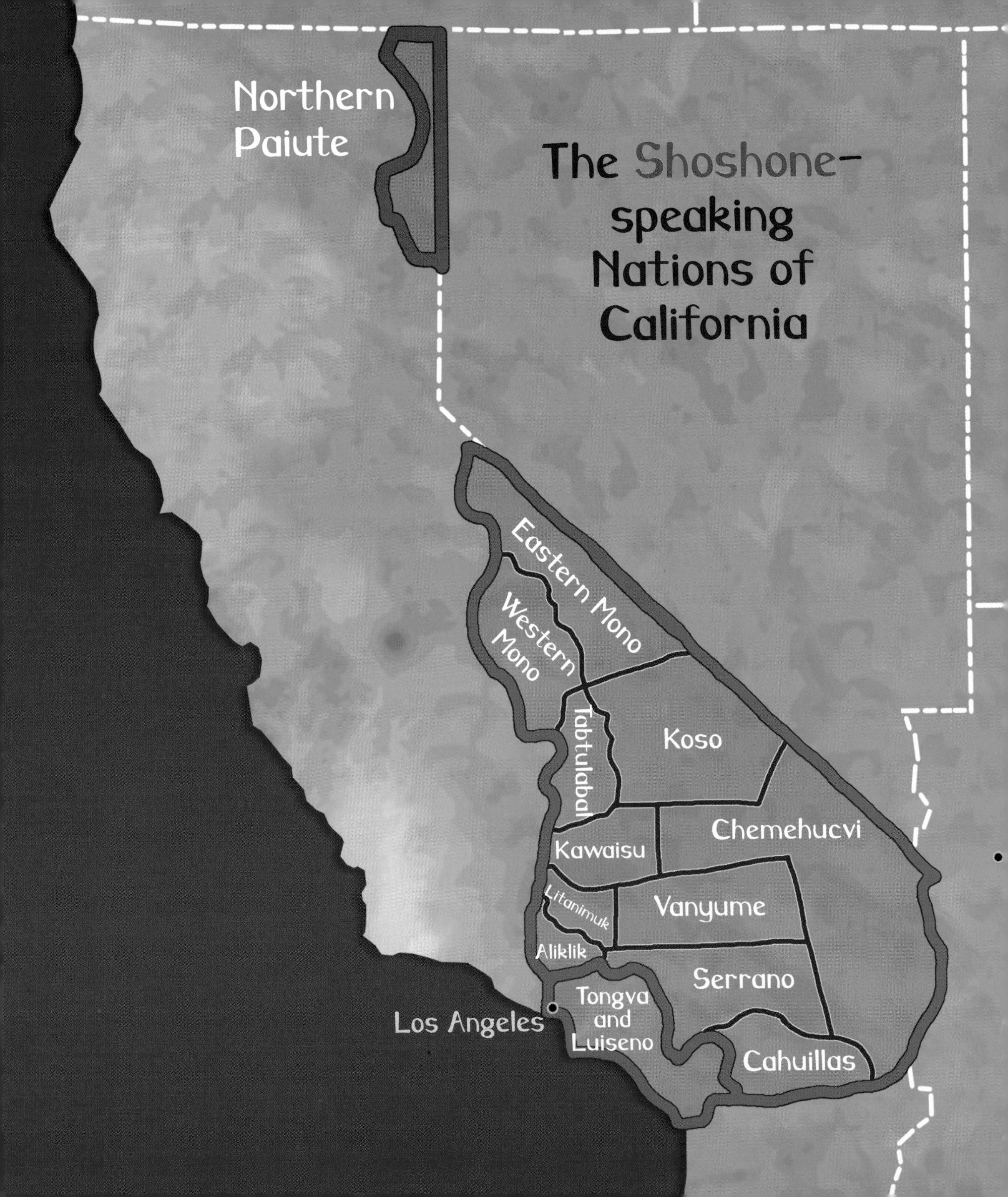

The Shoshone-speaking Nations of California

Northern Paiute

Eastern Mono

Western Mono

Tubtulabal

Koso

Chemehucvi

Kawaisu

Litanimuk

Vanyume

Aliklik

Serrano

Tongva and Luiseno

Los Angeles

Cahuillas

The Shoshone people made their home in this land of extreme contrasts. They represented a large group of independent nations who shared similar Uto-Aztecan languages.

No one knows exactly how many people lived in the Shoshone territory. Most experts agree that the region had a smaller population than the coastal areas of California or the enormous Central Valley that lay to the west of the Sierra Nevada mountain chain. Even today, relatively small numbers of people live in this part of California. The total population of the many Shoshone nations probably numbered in the tens of thousands. The size of the territory they occupied was very large. All in all, about a third of the modern state of California was inhabited by these peoples.

The origins of the word "Shoshone" have been lost to time. The native groups who share this language family have been divided into many different nations, or groups, with names such as the Northern Paiute, the Western Mono (also known as the Monache), the Pass Cahuilla, the Mountain Cahuilla, and the Desert Cahuilla. The names of the individual Shoshone nations come from native as well as Spanish and English place names and descriptive terms.

The Shoshone nations of the California interior shared many things besides language. They had similar religions and similar ways of making and using things. Taken together, the Shoshone people had an amazing ability to live off a seemingly uninhabitable land. Using their tremendous creative energy, some of these Native American groups have survived the challenges of the modern world.

This map shows the northern and southern territories of the Shoshone people in California.

Two

Origins

No one is certain where the Shoshone people came from. No one kept written records during the period in which their ancestors first appeared. However, archaeologists have worked with linguistic anthropologists, who investigate how languages are created and change over time. Together they have developed a picture of the origins and movement of the Shoshone nations.

Most scholars believe that the first inhabitants of the Americas arrived sometime between 13,000 and 40,000 years ago. The ancestors of all the Native American nations came from Asia using a narrow land bridge made up of ice and pockets of land. This land bridge spanned the gap between the continents of Asia and North America. Over time, groups of hunters moved farther and farther south, following herds of grazing animals. Over many centuries or perhaps thousands of years, some of these people developed the Shoshone language. In time, the Shoshone speakers spread over a very large part of North America, stretching from southern California to Wyoming and from Idaho to Texas.

Sometime around 1500 BC, some of the Shoshone people began to move to the south and west. By 1000 BC, the ancestors of the western Shoshone nations had settled into the region that

For thousands of years the Shoshone culture would flourish. This Shoshone woman with her baby wears typical dress from around the turn of the twentieth century.

today is known as Nevada. Their journeys to the south and west eventually brought them into the southeastern part of California. Some of the people moved on. Other groups also migrated from their first homeland. By 500 BC, repeated waves of the Shoshone

Thousands of years ago, a land bridge connected North America and Asia. This allowed early man to migrate in search of food and other resources. This map shows the routes that early man most likely took to arrive in the American West.

people had occupied the land from the coast of southern California to Nevada. They slowly took over, or absorbed, the people who already lived in these areas. No one can say if the Shoshone fought with other Native Americans who already lived in what would become their territory. No one really knows why some Shoshone decided to move. They may have relocated because of droughts, seeking lands with more food and water.

Many native people disagree with the archaeologists and linguistic anthropologists. They believe that their nations were created at the places where they were found when Europeans first arrived in California in the sixteenth century.

Archaeologists carefully uncover fragile pieces of the Shoshone past. Their findings can put together lost parts of Shoshone history.

Three
Daily Life

When Europeans first began to visit the Shoshone nations of eastern and southern California, they could not understand how these Native Americans were able to survive. The land seemed untamed and rugged, nearly impossible to live off of. To many outsiders, the Shoshones' jewelry, clothing, tools, religion, and houses looked like they belonged to another "more primitive" world. The ways the native people found food and shelter were also very different from those of the newcomers.

Living in a Hostile Land

Because of the harsh landscape in which they lived, the Shoshone people faced many challenges. Probably the most serious problem they faced was the frequent shortage of water. In a wet year, there could be as much as six times the amount of food that was available during a dry year. As a result, the Shoshone tried to take advantage of as many different food sources as possible. During a drought, their willingness to eat anything that they could often meant the difference between life and death. Women and children were normally assigned to gather wild plants, while the men did most of the hunting.

The Shoshone lived closely with their widely varying landscape. This photo captures the dramatic scenery of the Zabriskie Point Badlands in the Shoshone territory.

The land had many different kinds of animals and plants that could be eaten. The mountains and deserts were home to bighorn sheep, deer, bears, pronghorn antelope, and many other mammals that could be hunted for food. The lakes and streams of the higher elevations were filled with many kinds of fish. Smaller creatures, including birds, rats, mice, lizards, insects, and snakes, also found their way into Shoshone meals. There were also hundreds of different kinds of appetizing nuts, wild seeds, and

Much of the landscape in the Shoshone world was harsh and rugged. This woman and child were members of the Northern Paiute in Nevada.

edible roots, including wild onions. Some Shoshone communities, such as the Tübatulabal, were especially fond of keeping pets. The live animals found in their villages included young coyotes, geese, hawks, condors, and crows. The people of nearly all the Native American nations kept dogs.

The deserts had many other special food resources. The high deserts were filled with sagebrush and cedars. The lower deserts had less vegetation, but there were plenty of palm trees and cacti. The desert peoples ate mesquite beans, screwbeans, cactus pads, and fruit, as well as many kinds of wild seeds. Agave cacti grew in some areas. The roots of these spiny plants were roasted and eaten. In other places, spring rains produced desert surfaces that were covered with wild-flowers and grasses. These areas attracted immense numbers of small animals, such as rabbits, that depended on the plants for food. Shoshone people often formed large teams to hunt these creatures.

Pine nuts were a valuable food source for the Shoshone.

The mountains held many other special resources. In sharp contrast with the deserts, there were usually great supplies of water and trees. In some places, mushrooms, wild berries, grapes, and other wild fruit were abundant. For most Shoshone people, pine nuts represented one of the most important native foods. In the western region of North America, many Native Americans depended on acorns for a large part of their diet.

The most valuable areas within the Shoshone territory were the ones that bordered the deserts and mountains. Here, the climate varied much less than it did in the high country or the lower deserts. Therefore, the Shoshone people did not have to move as often or as great a distance in search of food, water, and other necessities.

Even in the locations with better weather and land, it was hard to find enough food to live in one place for the whole year. During different seasons, various kinds of plants and animals became abundant in different places. Most of the Shoshone people made a long journey in order to visit the various regions where food became plentiful. The summers were generally spent in the cooler parts of the mountain foothills, and the winters were spent in the areas that bordered the warmer deserts. Before the early 1800s, the Shoshone did not have horses. Instead, they had to haul everything on their backs. The constant movement made it impossible for the Shoshone to accumulate things that they could not carry with them.

Villages and Camps

The Shoshone people lived on the move. The largest camps or villages rarely had more than fifty people. The smallest communities were made up of single families. These people constantly roamed through their territory in order to find the food and water they needed. The small groups gathered together once or twice a year, when plants, such

This photo was taken near Pyramid Lake, Nevada, in the Northern Paiute territory. The Northern Paiute occupied an area that embraced much of northern Nevada and southern Oregon, along with a small part of east central California.

as pine nuts, or animals, such as rabbits, were abundant. The people who lived closer to more plentiful resources moved the least and therefore had the largest settlements.

The basic Shoshone house was made with a round or oval floor plan, in the shape of a cone or dome. The walls were made using things that were found close to their campsites. Wooden poles were used with rocks, bark, reeds, grass, branches, or similar clusters of brush. When they could find them, the Shoshone also found shelter in caves. The family homes were rarely more than 10 feet (3 m) in diameter. Most houses were equipped with a central fire pit used for cooking and heating. The roof of the house usually had a hole that allowed smoke to escape and sunlight to brighten the interior.

Some Shoshone people, including the Kitanemuk, built larger structures that provided both a community gathering place and protection against outsiders. A series of one-room homes were built side by side, encircling a plaza, or an open area. Each dwelling had its own fire pit and doorway that led to the plaza. Warriors guarded the one or two entrances that led into the enclosure. This kind of protected village was especially well suited to defend against enemies.

In areas where acorns were abundant, the Shoshone people built tiny storerooms on top of wooden platforms. These structures had walls made out of branches that were laced together. Most of the Shoshone people also used pits covered with dirt to store grains and nuts.

Most of the Shoshone groups had sweat houses. These were special types of buildings that were partially buried in the ground. In the middle of the room, there was a fire that filled the chamber with intense heat and smoke. The largest sweat houses were big enough for people to stand up in. The men often took sweat baths for spiritual purposes as well as part of healing ceremonies. Some men took sweat baths when they went hunting. The night before they left, they would go into the sweat house and burn strong-smelling plants, such as sage. When the men came out, the deer and similar animals would not be able to smell them. This allowed the hunters to sneak up on the animals without being detected.

Cooking

Shoshone women were usually responsible for creating the family's meals. They prepared food using a wide variety of methods. Many of the local wild plants were ground into powder using stone tools, including slablike metates and rocks with round basins, called mortars. In order to grind the food, the women used fist-size stones called manos and cylinder-shaped stones called pestles. The grinding tools were also used to tenderize tough meat.

All the Shoshone people made a wonderful array of cooking baskets. In order to heat food, the Shoshone placed small heated stones in the baskets with the food. In the southern and western areas, the Shoshone made strong pottery that was used in a similar manner.

While most of their meals were prepared over an open flame, some Shoshone groups also used cooking pits to roast food. They would dig a deep hole in the ground and build a hot fire that would be allowed to burn for several hours. The fuel was then removed from the pit.

The native chefs would place meat or vegetables wrapped in leaves in the center of the hole. The pit was then covered with additional earth. After a few hours, they would dig out the food, which was by this time piping hot and ready to eat. Even pinecones could be cooked using this method. The cones contained tasty nuts. After the initial roasting and shelling, they could be toasted on woven trays. Most of the pine nuts were then ground into flour using a metate and mono or a mortar and pestle.

This Shoshone woman, a Northern Paiute, uses a traditional method to clean pine nuts.

If someone wanted to preserve meat for later use, it would be smoked on a wooden rack. A small fire would be built under this structure. The meat was cut into thin strips and then placed on the device. After a few hours, the dried smoked meat was ready for storage.

Many of the native dishes were served in the form of a stew or porridge. Some of the food that the Shoshone found, such as wild berries, cactus fruit, and clover, could be eaten without any additional preparation.

Many Shoshone communities came together when food was abundant. Major harvests of acorns or pine nuts or massive rabbit hunts were usually followed by feasts and special ceremonies. This was one time of year when people enjoyed themselves and were able to dance and talk with their relatives and friends.

Because larger animals were usually hard to find, almost every part of the animal was used. The bones were cracked open to get the remaining bone marrow. The bones were also sometimes ground into a powder that was mixed with other foods. Blood was either drunk or cooked into cakes. Nothing was wasted.

21

Clothing and Body Decoration

The Shoshone's migration patterns kept them in relatively warm regions. As a result, most men and children wore very little clothing. In some regions, the men wore small pieces of deerskin suspended from their belts. These garments are called breechclouts. The Shoshone women generally covered the lower parts of their bodies with skirts or aprons. A few of the Shoshone communities made use of yucca or similar fibers for sandals. When it was cold, everyone used blankets or capes made from fur or leather to stay warm. The men and women of many groups wore tattoos or jewelry, including shell beads, bone and feather earrings, and similar pendants. Some Shoshone men used white paint to disguise their legs during hunting, allowing them to blend in to their surroundings. Nearly all the native communities emphasized the need for cleanliness. They frequently bathed in streams and lakes.

22   This Shoshone woman poses with necklaces in Owens Valley, California. The Shoshone were known for creating decorative jewelry.

Arts and Crafts

The Shoshone people produced many beautiful and practical items for everyday use. They had to rely on the natural resources that they found to create these items. The men modified stones to make dozens of different kinds of tools. Many of the objects that required sharp edges were made by chipping pieces of obsidian, flint, basalt, and similar rocks. The items they produced included spear-heads, knives, arrowheads, drills, and scrapers. Other stone tools were made by grinding the surfaces of pieces of rock. The heavier items, like metates and mortars, were often left in place when the community moved to a new location.

Smaller ground stone objects that were made by the Shoshone people included smoking pipes and arrow shaft straighten-ers. Among the southern Shoshone, straighteners were made from a special kind of rock known as steatite. Most rocks break apart if you put them in a fire. However, steatite does not break or crumble. The

The Shoshone made many types of beautiful and practical objects by using things they found in the natural world that surrounded them.

steatite straighteners could be heated in a fire before being used. The warmth enabled the arrows to be straightened quickly and efficiently.

The Shoshone women were expert basket makers. They produced dozens of different kinds of items. The baskets they made were shaped like jars, fans, dishes, bowls, trays, caps, and even boxes.

The Shoshone would carry much of their culture into the changing world of the twentieth century. This photograph of a Luiseño woman, seen here with traditional Shoshone baskets, was taken in 1901 near San Diego, California.

Certain kinds of special grasses, rushes, and tree shoots were collected and woven together using many different patterns. By alternating the materials, the craftswomen could produce interesting designs. Some baskets were woven so tightly that they could even hold liquids.

In the south and west, some Shoshone groups made pottery. Clay was taken from the hills and streambeds. The dry material was combined with sand and water, and then formed into long, snake-shaped pieces. The solid clay tubes were slowly coiled together to form containers. The sides of the objects were then smoothed using small round stones and wooden paddles. Every piece had to be carefully dried before it was stacked together with wood and brush. Finally the pile of wood and brush was set on fire and allowed to cook for many hours. Once the pottery had thoroughly cooled and hardened, it was put to use in storage or cooking.

The plant world provided the raw ingredients for many other Shoshone crafts. The bark of some trees and certain kinds of rushes and grasses were beaten to make a rough cloth that could be used for skirts. Wood was turned into digging sticks, musical instruments, clubs, throwing sticks (for hunting), mortars and pestles, arrow shafts, spears, bowls, cups, house poles, ladles, stirring sticks, and trays. Some Shoshone people crafted wooden bowls and trays that were decorated with pieces of carved seashells. Some plants, including agave cactus, milkweed, and yucca, could be used to make strong threads or cords. The strands could be woven together to fashion nets, bags, belts, and similar items. Some of the Shoshone people who lived in areas with lakes created small, simple boats by tying bundles of reeds together.

The animal world offered other important resources. Furs and skins became skirts, aprons, bags, ropes, belts, and blankets. Important items that were made out of bone included awls, flutes, combs, beads, gaming sticks, hairpins, needles, saws, and hammers.

Shoshone craftspeople incorporated bird feathers into headdresses, special skirts, and arrows. Some northern groups made elaborate headbands from porcupine quills. The sinews, or tendons, taken from deer were used to make powerful bowstrings.

Although the Shoshone were not farmers, they often made changes in their environment to encourage the growth of wild plants. For example,

The porcupine is a familiar creature in the Shoshone world. Quills from these animals were used to make headbands.

they burned off certain natural areas that contained unwanted plants. This method would increase the growth of useful grasses, such as those that produced seeds that could be eaten.

Trade

Although the Shoshone people made most of the things that they used, a relatively small number of items were acquired through trade. These objects included certain kinds of stones that were used to make chipped tools, such as arrowheads. Some trade goods were acquired from the coastal people, including the Chumash and the Tongva. The Shoshone valued shell beads and pendants. Some groups also traded for tools made from a combination of wood and shell, along with garments made from sea mammal skins.

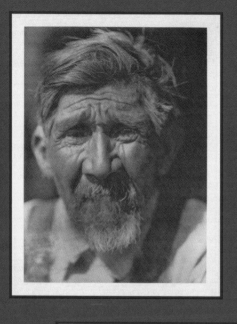

Four

Other Aspects of Shoshone Life

Among the Shoshone, membership in various groups was based on whether a person was a man or a woman, how much wealth that person had, his or her age, and who his or her parents were.

The smallest social unit was the family. The oldest male was usually in charge. Marriages were often arranged by parents, and in some Shoshone groups, husbands were allowed to change wives. In the areas with more resources, several families were sometimes joined together to form a clan. These people all claimed to have had a common animal ancestor, such as a wildcat or coyote. Several clans living together in the same place were sometimes combined to form two moieties, or family units. The largest social unit of the Shoshone people was the village or local community. No one thought of themselves in terms of nations or regional groups. Each of the social divisions helped to regulate work assignments and relations within society.

Among many larger Shoshone communities, there were overall political leaders, or chiefs. These men were sometimes allowed to have up to three wives. The chiefs received many gifts from their people. However, they were expected to distribute these objects during times of crisis or religious celebrations. In some communities, the right to be chief was handed down from father to son.

There were many faces of the Shoshone world. Shoshone-speaking nations were active throughout much of the American West, from Idaho to the southern coast of California.

Occasionally, when there was no son, the honor was handed down to a daughter. In many villages a chief was selected on the basis of his knowledge and abilities.

Most of the Shoshone people thought of themselves as equals. They owned similar amounts of things. Because of the need to keep moving, few chiefs were able to amass much wealth. However, some of the larger groups who did not have to move as frequently were able to accumulate more property. For example, after a war, captives were sometimes divided among the warriors, who would force the captives into slavery. These slaves were forced to work hard, and they were not given the same benefits as other people.

Most Shoshone communities also had a number of people who served as part-time religious leaders and doctors. These individuals collected sacred objects that were believed to hold special powers. Some of these powers were given to the doctors by spirits, or ancestors, during unusual dreams. The Shoshone doctors were respected members of their societies. Some of these people were also feared because many Shoshone believed the doctors could use their skills to harm, as well as help, people.

Government

The basic unit of government was the village. Every settlement had a chief, who helped to regulate many aspects of daily life. In the more populated regions, each community also controlled the areas where it collected resources. Anyone who came into the village lands had to get permission from the chief, or the visitor could be attacked. The chief was often asked to decide the outcomes of disputes between families. The chief also provided leadership during wars. None of the chiefs had absolute power, and they almost always led by example. The members of their families sometimes aided the chief by serving as messengers and advisers.

Warfare

The Shoshone people usually went to war because they were being attacked or they felt that they had to defend resources that belonged to their village. The Shoshone rarely sent people out on expeditions to capture their neighbors' property or make them prisoners. Among the southern groups, there were traditional alliances that combined the strengths of the Chemehuevi, Southern Paiute, Quechan (Yuma), Kamia, Yavapai, and

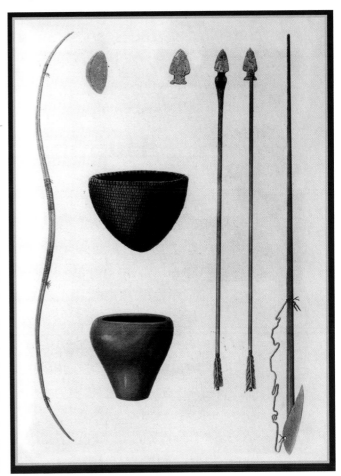

Even weapons came from the natural world that surrounded the Shoshone. These bows and arrows were made of wood and stone by expert Shoshone craftspeople.

Western Apache. When a village suffered a raid or had some of its people captured, it had no choice but to respond. When they went to fight, the men were led into battle by the village chief. The warriors relied on bows and arrows and spears in combat. In southern California, the Shoshone communities also used a wooden club with a large head, as well as poisoned arrows. After Europeans introduced horses in the 1800s, some Shoshone groups used them to raid their enemies. The people who lived in the areas where food and water were scarce were mostly unable to fight. They had to devote all their efforts to basic survival.

Hunting and Fishing

The Shoshone people hunted most of the animals and insects that they ate. The most common weapon used for hunting was the bow and arrow. Some Shoshone groups also used spears, nets, snares, and L-shaped throwing sticks. The smaller weapons were especially useful in rabbit hunts. Many hunters wore deerskins and antler headdresses as disguises. Other individuals used fire to force small animals into restricted areas where they could be shot with arrows or clubbed. Many Shoshone people built hiding places near trails using brush or rocks. When large animals, such as deer, came near, the hunters would shoot them with their bows and arrows.

The Shoshone nations that lived near rivers, streams, and lakes developed many methods for fishing. In some areas, they relied on nets. In other places they used spears or arrows. Some communities built small dams in shallow waters to divert fish into baskets or brush traps.

Language

The Shoshone people's languages belong to the larger Uto-Aztecan language group. Each Shoshone language group can be further divided into numerous local dialects, or regional variations. Unfortunately, many of these dialects and languages disappeared before they could be recorded. Modern Shoshone speakers from different regions can generally understand each other. For example, Shoshone people from southern California can easily be understood by their distant cousins, the Comanche, who traditionally lived in southern Colorado and Texas.

Religion

Although the Shoshone people had a number of similar religious practices, each nation also had unique religious beliefs. Despite their differences, their beliefs helped them to make sense of the world that they lived in. Their religion also taught them important lessons about what it took to be a good person.

Most of the Shoshone's religious celebrations were tied to times of harvest. On these occasions, the people often offered thanks for their

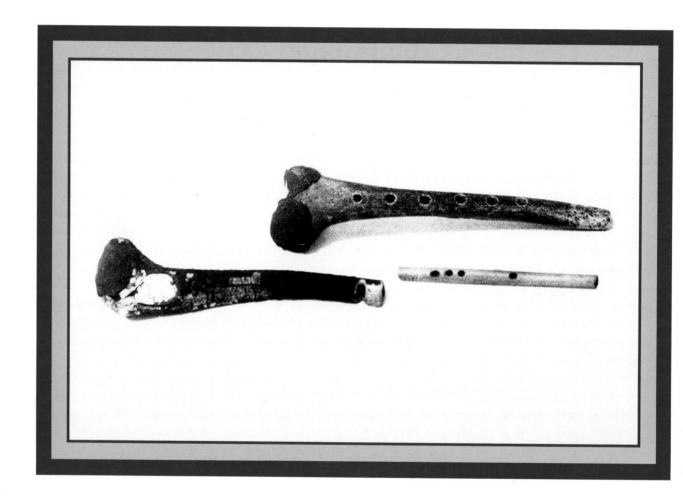

34 These Tongva musical instruments were created from animal bone and were used for both religious and recreational purposes. The Tongva were one of the Shoshone-speaking coastal nations whose territory included modern-day Los Angeles.

survival or asked for the help of supernatural forces. Other rituals marked the various stages of life that a person passes through from birth to death. A great deal of time was spent learning community traditions and history. Many ceremonies were held in order to keep the Shoshone's lives, and world, in balance.

When the Shoshone worshipped, they often sang and danced. Human voices provided the music. Some southern California people used flutes, panpipes, clappers, and rattles as instruments. The same groups used strings equipped with weights that were whirled in the air to create a roaring sound. The religious leaders often wore special body paint, clothing, and headdresses. In some groups, the people in each clan wore special patterns of facial paint. In some Shoshone communities, special plants were boiled into a soup that helped young people have sacred dreams where they could learn from spirits.

Many Shoshone had elaborate funerals. Most of the groups buried their dead, although some communities that lived in southern California burned the bodies. Sometimes, the property of the dead was burned over their graves. An additional funeral was usually held one year after someone died. Songs and dances were believed to help the spirit of a dead person on his or her journey through the afterlife.

Most Shoshone communities marked the faces of rocky places with symbols or other designs. Sometimes these images were painted. This type of decoration is known as a pictograph. Other designs were scratched into the face of the rocks. This type of image

36 Many animals were considered sacred to the Shoshone-speaking nations. Feathered charms, like the one pictured here, were used by the Cahuilla for religious purposes.

is called a petroglyph. We do not understand why the Shoshone people made this rock art. Many people believe that the pictures were made as part of a religious ceremony. Because rock art is sacred to many modern Native Americans, it is essential that people show respect when they view them.

The Shoshone have many different religious stories. One famous Chemehuevi belief involves their origins. According to some religious leaders, Coyote and his elder brother, Puma, built a home on a high mountain peak, now known as Charleston Peak, when the world was covered with water. The old woman of the west, Hawichyepa Maapuch, made the land dry out. Coyote searched for people but could not find any. He married a sacred bug who then laid eggs. These eggs hatched into many native nations, including the Chemehuevi. As Coyote's family grew, it faced many challenges. After the death of Puma, Coyote put together the sacred funeral rituals that are still observed by traditional people.

The first Europeans who reached the land that would become California arrived in 1540. During the 200 years that followed, many Spanish explorers visited the coast. In 1769, the first European colony was created at San Diego. However, during the entire period from 1540 to 1769, nearly all the Shoshone people lived far away from the regions where foreigners were seen.

Despite the fact that few newcomers actually came into contact with the Shoshone people of the interior, they still influenced the Native Americans. Although they did not understand or intend it, Europeans unleashed a wide variety of diseases into California. While no records for this period exist, it is very probable that these diseases, such as measles and smallpox, killed many Native Americans, just as they did in other parts of North America. In many regions, the population was reduced by as much as 90 percent.

The Shoshone and Spanish California

Between 1769 and 1821, Spain developed a series of missions and military bases (presidios) along the coast of California. Although the

After hundreds of years of living peacefully, the Shoshone would see great changes during the eighteenth and nineteenth centuries. The result would be many bloody conflicts between Native Americans and the European newcomers.

Spanish wanted to build more settlements in the interior, the Shoshone people remained outside of the area under European political control.

The first visitor to the Shoshone region was probably the soldier Pedro Fages. He passed through the western boundary of the Shoshone territory in southern California in 1772. Two years later, another soldier, Juan Bautista de Anza, crossed through a small portion of the Cahuilla territory as he made his way from Tucson, Arizona, to the coastal settlement of Monterey. Anza returned in 1775 with a group of colonists who would later found the settlement of San Francisco. The next year, Father Francisco Garcés, a Franciscan from Arizona, reached the Chemehuevi area of southern California. He was the first missionary to take an interest in establishing outposts in the interior.

Despite the fact that they had little direct contact with the newcomers, the natives' lives were affected by the new people in several ways. Many of the old trading relations with coastal peoples were brought to an

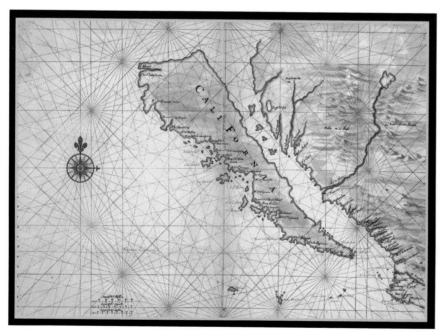

California was one of the last regions of North America to be thoroughly explored by Europeans. Before 1750, many mapmakers showed California as a large island.

end, and the introduction of new diseases killed many Shoshone. Newly introduced animals and plants spread from the coast into the interior, often doing terrible damage to the environment. Native plants and grasses that were important to the Shoshone began to disappear.

Although the new era brought many hardships, such as disease, it also brought new things to the Shoshone. Some Shoshone people took up the use of tobacco, which was often chewed with powdered lime. The native people did not know that tobacco caused diseases, and they enjoyed its flavor and its effect as a stimulant. Other groups experimented with growing crops and even created irrigation systems. Where there was grass and water, sheep, horses, cattle, and mules found their way into the interior. Many coastal Native Americans fled the mission system and joined Shoshone communities in the interior. They brought with them many foreign tools, foods, and customs, as well as new ideas about growing plants and

Not everything the newcomers brought to the Shoshone was bad. The Europeans brought horses, which the Shoshone were able to tame and ride. This would vastly improve the Shoshone way of life, allowing for better methods in hunting and warfare.

raising animals. Soon the Native Americans began to experiment with the introduced technologies.

The horse was probably the most important item that moved from the coast into the interior during this period. The Shoshone who had access to enough water and grass to support the animals soon found that they were extremely useful. Horses made it possible to move large amounts of baggage in a way that would have been unimaginable in earlier times.

Additionally, horses made it possible to fight more effectively in war. This became increasingly important. The Mojave people who lived to the southeast of the Chemehuevi soon began to attack Shoshone settlements. The Mojave had already mastered the new fighting techniques on horseback. Many prisoners were taken and turned into slaves who were sold to other Native Americans or Spaniards in southern Arizona. There were also times when it seemed like the foreigners from the coast might invade the Shoshone region. In 1819, some southern California Shoshone were caught in the middle of a war being fought by the Mojave and the Spaniards.

The Shoshone and the Mexican Republic

By 1821, many of the Shoshone's lives had been forever changed by the introduction of horses, new diseases, and European technologies and customs. While the old trading patterns had collapsed, dangerous new alliances were being formed by Native Americans and newcomers that threatened many Shoshone communities.

Between 1821 and 1831, the number of non-native people who visited the Shoshone country steadily increased. Most of these visitors arrived from the east. They included fur trappers from the United States as well as Hispanic settlers from New Mexico. The New Mexicans

The Mexican-American War would turn parts of the Shoshone land into a battlefield. America's victory in the war would bring much of the Southwest into the United States's possession.

arrived in the deserts of southern California in search of trading opportunities. They came by the way of a new route, which was called the Old Spanish Trail. This route passed through the center of the Shoshone territory in southern California. The New Mexicans came to trade with the Native Americans in the interior. They exchanged wool blankets, beads, knives, and other metalwares for mules and horses. Many groups living in the interior captured these animals in raids that were undertaken against the coastal settlements.

By 1840, an emerging belt of ranches was extending Mexican control almost to the coast of southern California. Some Serrano people found jobs in these new settlements. They soon mastered the Spanish language, and many began to adopt Roman Catholic religious beliefs. Some Serrano were able to mix their new lifestyle with traditional hunting and gathering.

By the time of the Mexican-American War (1846–1847), it was getting harder and harder for many Shoshone living in the south to continue traditional lifestyles. A time of change was about to begin that would further fragment, and ultimately devastate, the Shoshone world.

The Shoshone and the Americans

The transfer of the territory of California from Mexico to the United States brought a new series of invasions into the Shoshone region. The discovery of gold in the Sierra Nevada mountains in 1849 brought immense numbers of newcomers to California. As soon as the gold gave out in the area of the original discoveries, the miners began to move in search of new treasure. This time, it would be the Shoshone-speaking Native Americans living in the northern end of the state who would be hit first.

Those natives who were unlucky enough to live in a region where gold was discovered suffered the most. In many cases whole villages were simply destroyed to make way for gold mines. In other places, the Native Americans were forced to live as beggars or as slaves. The miners' pollution of land and water did terrible damage

This illustration depicts a small mining town during the California gold rush. The gold rush would spell doom for the traditional Shoshone way of life in California. No laws and no guns could protect the natives as greedy prospectors ravaged the California landscape.

to the delicate mountain and desert environments. Additionally, new diseases, spread by close interaction with the newcomers, killed many Native Americans.

Additional waves of invasion came about as major trails and, later, railroads passed through the Shoshone territory. As early as 1849, a new road was created that connected Los Angeles with Salt Lake City, Utah. Less than a decade later, passengers crossed Shoshone territory on the Butterfield Stage Line. New towns that grew up on native lands at places like Bodie, Cerro Gordo, and Palm Springs were created without any concern for the fact that the land was already the property of Shoshone communities. A chain of United States Army forts, such as Fort Independence, Fort Paiute, Fort Cody, and Fort Jurupa, were established to protect the newcomers and prevent violence between immigrants and natives.

In 1850, Governor Peter Burnett declared that all Native Americans in California should be forced to live like Europeans or killed if they refused. Although not all the newcomers agreed, few were willing to work toward building better relations with Native Americans. By the last decade of the nineteenth century, it was clear that the Shoshone faced a future of racism, poverty, discrimination, and disease.

When Shoshone leaders attempted to form treaties with the invaders, they were almost always misled and ultimately betrayed. The lands that were set aside by government officials for Native Americans were usually stolen by settlers. Wealthy

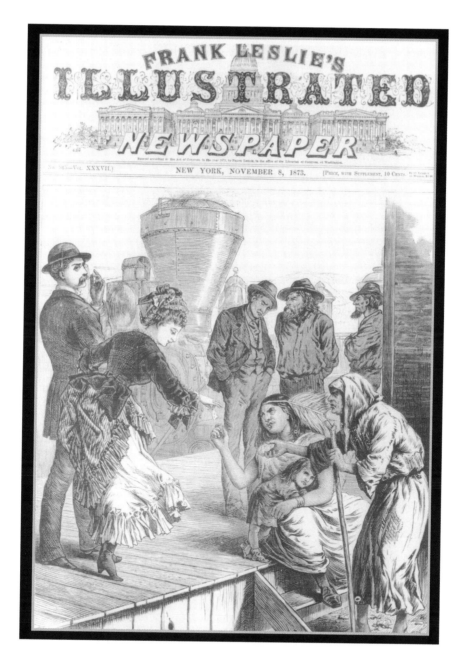

During the gold rush, boomtowns sprang up after gold was discovered. Wealthy people would move in and force the Native Americans out of their land and into poverty. This illustration shows Native American women begging for money from wealthy white Americans.

speculators took advantage of laws that discriminated against the native nations, who were treated as if they, and not the invaders, were foreigners. If the Native Americans refused to go to the filthy prisons the settlers called "reservations," they were labeled dangerous renegades and were often shot on sight. The court system protected the newcomers from any punishment.

Only a small number of Shoshone children had a chance to get a formal education. It was not until after 1880 that the first school for Native Americans opened its doors. When it did, the children were often taught that the native way of life was bad or simply wrong. Students were not allowed to speak their native languages, and they were often forced to live away from their parents. During vacation periods, many students were required to work for local settlers as a way of raising more money to run the schools. Some of the children who made their homes in the more remote places were kidnapped by settlers and raised as servants. Some newcomers even began to capture Native American children and sell them as slaves. By 1865, a Native American child was worth anywhere from $50 to $100. It was not until 1867 that the United States government began to put an end to this abuse. Even then, vicious settlers found ways to keep their native prisoners as forced laborers.

During this terrible time of desperation, a Shoshone spiritual leader named Wovoka began to preach a new set of religious beliefs. He came from the community that lived in Walker Pass. Wovoka had a vision that the Native Americans could get back their lands and return to their old traditions through special rituals. In 1869, he began to preach his nonviolent message of native revival. His ideas quickly spread to the east and west, to many non-Shoshone groups. Unfortunately, Wovoka's peaceful views were eventually turned into a call for violent resistance by some native

Wovoka *(seated)* would inspire many Native American tribes in the late 1880s. He imagined peace and a world without white men. Sadly, his message was no match for westward expansion.

leaders. The war that resulted created misunderstanding and retaliation by American government officials who mistakenly felt that the message of Wovoka was one of hatred.

Other Shoshone community leaders who sought to resist the onslaught were punished or killed. As the population of newcomers grew, more and more native lands were stolen. A new law issued by the state government of California in 1850 made it possible for any newcomer to declare a Native American a "vagrant." He or she could then be taken as a prisoner and forced to work like a slave. Special taxes were placed on native lands. Juan Antonio Garra, a southern California Shoshone, organized a revolt in the south in 1851 that was ruthlessly crushed. Garra was executed by a shot to the head. During the months that followed the uprising, many of the settlers killed innocent Native Americans.

As the decades progressed, more and more of the Shoshone people were treated as if they were not even human beings. When some newcomers who disagreed with the majority tried to stop the abuses, they were told that these Native Americans didn't count. The racist Americans said they did not have any rights, because they were only "digger Indians," a term used to portray the Shoshone as lazy and stupid. Despite the racial hatred, a small but growing group of settlers did form friendships with Native Americans. Some non-native men married Native American women.

After 1860, the surviving Shoshone who lived closest to the settlers adopted more and more traits that they felt were useful. For example, adobe homes with grass roofs were adopted in place of traditional housing among the Cahuilla. Nearly all the Shoshone found that European-style clothing, along with iron and steel tools, met many of their practical needs.

It was not until the early twentieth century that things began to significantly improve for the Shoshone. However, progress was slow. Many native people served with distinction in World War I. As a result, the United States granted citizenship to all Native Americans in 1924. Shoshone leaders renewed their fights to keep their lands and to gain control over their children's educations. After 1930, more and more of the government's policies helped, rather than hurt, the native survivors.

A surprising amount of the traditional Shoshone lands in eastern and southern California remains much as it has since 1500. However, most of the communities that greeted newcomers from Spain, Mexico, and the United States have disappeared. A few Shoshone nations still continue to live in their traditional territories on reservations. Like most Native Americans, the surviving Shoshone groups' lifestyle has significantly changed in response to the modern world. By the year 2000, they had adopted most of the characteristics of the rest of the American population.

Many of the surviving Shoshone nations are working hard to gain the recognition that they deserve. Most Native Americans feel that the United States has failed to live up to its treaty guarantees. Many native nations are also working hard to correct inaccurate or dishonest images of Native Americans seen on television, in the movies, and in classrooms. They want to be granted the civil rights given to other Americans. Despite more than a century of problems, they are committed to building a better future for their people as both Native Americans and citizens of the United States.

Rupert Costo, a Cahuilla who founded the American Indian Historical Society in 1964, is an example of the kind of individual

Today, the Shoshone continue to move forward while holding closely to their cultural past. This mural, located in Los Angeles, depicts Cahuilla culture along the California coast long before newcomers arrived.

54 Today, the Shoshone remain a strong and vibrant part of Native American culture in California. Joseph Ontiveros *(pictured)* helps to preserve ancient Tongva traditions as the curator of the Haramokngna Cultural Center at the Angeles National Forest.

who has worked hard to improve native lives. In 1973, he helped to start a Native American monthly newspaper called *Wassaja*. Besides his work as a scholar, Costo was also a longtime tribal chairman. His efforts have stood as a guiding force to other individuals who are interested in native rights and building a better world.

The people who made California's lands their homes have not disappeared. Although the Shoshone have overcome terrible hardships and cruelty, the struggle for justice continues. The resistance of Shoshone and other native nations has become an inspiration to the whole world.

Timeline

13,000– 40,000 years ago	The ancestors of the Shoshone nations arrive in North America from Asia.
6,000–8,000 years ago	Native peoples who are the ancestors of the Shoshone settle in the area of the modern state of Nevada.
3,500–5,000 years ago	Shoshone-speaking people move to the south and west, into what is today eastern and southern California.
1540–1769	Europeans explore areas near the Shoshone nations. They introduce diseases that are likely to have significantly reduced the size of the Shoshone population.
1769–1835	The Spanish and Mexican governments establish a chain of missions, towns, and military bases along the California coast.
1772	Pedro Fages skirts the western boundary of the territory of the Shoshone people of southern California.

Juan Bautista de Anza leads an expedition that crosses part of the southern Shoshone territory.

Father Francisco Garcés visits Shoshone people.

Increasing numbers of American fur trappers and merchants from New Mexico trade with Native Americans living in the interior, including the Shoshone people.

The United States gains California as a result of the Mexican-American War.

The gold rush begins in the Sierra Nevada. During the next half century, miners will invade much of the Shoshone territory. By the end of the era, the Shoshone people living close to the newcomers have few opportunities to continue traditional lifestyles or customs.

The Garra uprising in southern California ends in disaster.

All Native Americans are made U.S. citizens.

The image of Sacagawea, a Shoshone woman, is placed on a newly minted dollar coin. Sacagawea helped guide Lewis and Clark during their exploration of the American Northwest.

Glossary

alliance (uh-LY-uhntz) A partnership to further the common interests of the groups involved.

anthropologist (an-thruh-PAH-luh-jist) A researcher who investigates the cultural, social, and physical aspects of human life.

archaeologist (ark-e-AH-luh-jist) An anthropologist who specializes in the study of the relationship between the things people make and their activities. Most archaeologists focus their research on the past.

bedrock mortar (BED-rok MOR-tur) A large outcropping of stone with numerous holes, or round basins, where nuts and seeds were ground into flour.

drought (DROWT) A period of prolonged dryness that causes damage to crops.

irrigation (ih-rih-GAY-shun) To carry water to land through ditches or pipes.

linguistic anthropologist (lin-GWIHS-tik an-thruh-PAH-luh-jist) A researcher of anthropology who focuses on the study of languages.

mano (MAH-no) A fist-sized piece of stone that is used in combination with a metate to grind nuts and seeds into flour.

metate (me-TAH-tay) A slablike piece of stone with depressions that is used with a mano to grind seeds and nuts into flour.

migration (my-GRAY-shun) The movement of people or animals from one place to another.

mission system (MI-shon SIS-tem) A system used to spread religious beliefs to another country or religion

moieties (MOY-ah-teez) Social units representing one-half of a society that is based on a division according to family relations.

mortar (MOR-tur) A large stone with circular holes used to grind nuts and seeds into flour.

pestle (PEH-sul) A cylinder-shaped stone that is used with a mortar to grind nuts and seeds into flour.

petroglyph (PEH-truh-glif) Rock art that has designs created using scratching or carving.

pictograph (PIK-toh-graf) Rock art that has designs created using paint.

plunder (PLUN-der) To take by force.

racist (RAY-sist) One who believes one race is better than another.

rock art (ROK ART) A form of art that involves scratching, carving, or painting designs or pictures on large rock surfaces.

social structure (SOH-shul STRUK-chur) The way that a large group of people is divided into smaller groups.

speculators (SPEK-yoo-lay-terz) Those who assume business risks; often those searching for gold.

supernatural (soo-per-NA-chuh-ruhl) Not usual or normal; something that goes against the laws of nature.

transitional areas (tran-ZIH-shun-uhl EHR-ee-uhz) Geographic regions that lie along the boundary of deserts and mountains that have particularly desirable resources.

vegetation (ve-jah-TAY-shun) Plant life.

Resources

BOOKS

Campbell, Paul D. *Survival Skills of Native Californians.* Salt Lake City: Gibbs Smith, 1999.

Malinowski, Sharon, ed. *Gale Encyclopedia of Native American Tribes.* Detroit: Gale Group, 1998.

Rawl, James J. *Indians of California: The Changing Image.* Norman, OK: University of Oklahoma Press, 1986.

Stanley, Terry. *Digger: The Tragic Fate of the California Indians from the Missions to the Gold Rush.* New York: Crown Publishing/ Random House, 1997.

MUSEUMS

Nevada State Museum, Las Vegas
700 Twin Lakes Drive
Las Vegas, NV 89107
(702) 486-5205
Web site: http://dmla.clan.lib.nv.us/docs/museums/lv/vegas.htm

Phoebe A. Hearst Museum of Anthropology
103 Kroeber Hall, UC
Berkeley, CA 94720-3712
(510) 642-3682
e-mail: pahma@uclink4.berkeley.edu
Web site: http://hearstmuseum.berkeley.edu

Southwest Museum
234 Museum Drive
Los Angeles, CA 90065
(213) 221-2164
Web site: http://www.southwestmuseum.org

WEB SITES

Due to the changing nature of Internet links, The Rosen Publishing Group, Inc., has developed an online list of Web sites related to the subject of this book. This site is updated regularly. Please use this link to access the list:

http://www.rosenlinks.com/lnac/shos

Index